Novels by Jack Beltane:

The Toyland Tales:
    Am I the Matter?
    Three Dances
    In a Yellow Field

A Company of Tatters

Available from Graveworm Press

Nightshade & Daylight

poems by
Jack Beltane

Graveworm Press

Cleveland, Ohio

Nightshade & Daylight

Contents

People & Remembrances

Philosophy & Dreams

When the Moon is Watching the Still Earth

I must remember these things that make me human.
In my soft rush to get ahead
for a chance to be myself
I must stop and listen
for the sound of oars in still water,
the rolling toll of thunder on the wind,
the pleasing breath of birds' wings,
the lonely bark of a strange dog—

all these things glitter in a way
what I see cannot glimpse.
The truth of the matter betrays
the simple finds and fortunes that sparkle,
yet fade away to a background noise
of darkness that leaves me
with empty hands upturned to heaven as a cup.

These are the things I catch
when the moon is watching the still earth:
The stuff of memories and dreams;
the glowing breath of life.

Obsidian Pleasure

As each fell ocean churns over a new mountain,
so must each of us rely:
We must leave our homes intact.

All about us is a fog—amorphous
secrets and a place to spread our wings.
We are here and to here we shall return,
creeping slowly westward, ever toward the gloaming.
We but mar the surface,
leaving behind a few tattered structures.

We must become air, the very breath,
the vehicle of the stars—this that is
around us, neverending.
All life that passes
between its great, gentle fingers
pushes us to grandeur.

We are but lights in the darkness.
Let us burn now, for to the darkness
we must return.

There

When the rains fell even the broken clouds looked too blue—
the far starlight and the planets moving
like small bulbs in an empty room.

There was a sound—
the soft maw opened and it all rushed out. Later,
when the lights faded and the flashes dimmed,
the wind turned ceaselessly through the trees.

There was a cavern—
a place of soft mud and sand and
the toilsome silence of no sound.

There was a light—
a gentle play on shadows, a glimmer, a hope.

Then there was tomorrow.

The Dream of the Gray Wolf

Outside listening
to the merry mystic music
swaying in the wind before the storm.
Rain smells heavy in the air,
noisy with the breath of life.

Everything's stirring in this spring pool—
someone's slamming shutters,
dust dances on the roof,
the engines' cool soft hum
on the street below.

I lie here waiting for the rain to fall.
The air hangs around me
waiting to fall.

In bed between the crisp sheets
whispering
lingering—
another engine's growl.
The wind wilds fragrances of oil and gasoline.
My face is dampened—
the sky crying open over my head.

I vanish into my surroundings,
fall soundlessly through sheets
of memories billowed like sails,
waiting only to rise.

Again the cries of forward motion,
perpetual motion, will rise.

One house
solitary
below the clouds
spinning out of direction
up and up:
the street
the neighborhood
the valley
the hills
the cold eye of the sun above the clouds.

Can I follow the course of this river
all the way to New Orleans?
Hocking
Ohio
Mississippi
The Delta
River queen and voodoo mamma
are you all that you seem?
May I trouble you for a while—
I'm searching for a book.
A life.

But here and now
the gentle patter of the rain—
cleansing power or rebirth.

I dreamed I saw a gray wolf dying,
shrunken eyes and ribs,
caved-in belly.
I looked in its plaintive eyes unsettled—
perhaps I had been expected.
"I'm sorry!" I cried,
"What else could I do?"

The wolf lay down its head
saying nothing at all.

Butterfly Mechanics

Frozen green waves forever
threatening the valley shore
like forced, marching armies—
as far as I can imagine
they push their fingers in.
Their power welders; lies dormant;
needs some chance to reflect.

Far beyond is brightness:
The light about which these hills have kept
quiet for all long time,
spanning distances of cultures,
lying sanely in wait.

In the summer they said he was gone,
the small boy with the chapped lips.
I remember his mouth, shaped
like a mushroom or the cool oh of summer
beading sweat and insolence.

The dream replaces me now
like a silent memory
on the surface of a deep pool
charred by ripples and moved by
the breathing gills of fish,
where fat-bellied flies
doze in forgotten fields
like butterflies too afraid to move

for disturbing the air.

He showed me how to swim,
then he sank like a cold star and turned
me on toward oblivion.

There was something he whispered
about beauty and the need to see:
The purple-jet air breathed twilight
into the sky and moved quickly to pick up the ashes
of the falling bird that circled the heavens
like a disused cigarette on a spiral to the end.

The Thin Green Light

My days have run like stars
on top of a cold mountain.
I have traveled
between the dreams and echoes,
between the trees.

The light is a thin green swirling
in the air before the spirits of thunder
send down their voices on low
slender waves.

There are lands beyond these shores.
I have glimpsed them through the mists
like far off lights
caught in a web of sparkles.

Somewhere something glows
a cold harsh blue
beside the camera's eye,
yet none of this comes out on film.

All things passing pass through
this point of time.
Best to be ready.

Dogs' Teeth

We keep sharp thing around us
like dogs' teeth set in firm jaws
and minds of their own.

We keep prisoners in the silence
they have found as refuge from the world
and the sanity they betray.

We keep deep, dark lands no more,
fearing that over which
we do not dominate.

We face grim death
with every slow, thoughtful breath
we take.

Abandoned in Spirals

What soft music ceases now,
falls softly from petals of snow
like drifted wind?

Whence came all this noise,
all this clatter and bang to own
in a quiet still universe
spinning out further than we'll ever see?

When the rainbow lost its fire
and the colors dribbled slowly
down the sky,
where were you then,
when I needed you most?

Abandoned?
In my mind?
My eyes?
My lips that have
never known the soft remembrance
of your mouth on mine?

All this time—
these days stretched like pearls
on a necklace I made for you—
yet I have nothing to know for it.
No sparkling memories or charged dreams,
only this quiet—

this enduring sense of space
like the black spiral of the universe
that coils me
still further from you.

But I can taste the sunrise;
see music hanging in the air—
that must mean something.

What whispered sinister title
shall I give to you?
I know you, your moods:
You can only twist so far
before you will break.

And when the pieces shatter
and the old boots of humanity grind
them to dust,
who will come crawling from the woodwork
to find you and return
you to your glory?

Who will be there
to repaint the rainbow?

Answer me that and we shall go,
soft blossom to petal,
you and I through this sadness
we call life.

Until then I must see realism
from my pillow, for this future—
this colorless day called forever—
stretches on too far for my fingers
to snatch.

For now,
the soft music and your smile.

Tetra Obscura

I'm still afraid of thunder.
The lightning in her eyes calms me
like a cool wave of summer
flooding the senses with insects and
deep amber prisms of light washed through leaves—
dropped, scarlet, next to my bed
where the music plays on endlessly;
the bugs are just winding up the chorus.

On and on and on through the morning,
wee sleep and flowers opening like jaws
on a new day.
But here, endless rainbows,
slippers of time like honey
clinging to the shadows,
heaving in and out as stars pass—
the moon relights the day.

At last, the dream
escaping. With its passing comes shudders,
visions of mountain folds deep green with life
in valleys where rivers run unknown,
but to a few they are the world.

Alive.

I Have Made My Cross of Stone

I hurt for everyone else.
My mind twists into shapes distorted
by the view through the rain.

I am pulled again,
sliding easily down a wet panel of glass,
my fingers dragging along, squeaking,
leaving trails of water behind
my nails that beg for purchase.
Yet they can never be
long enough.

I whisper to the words calling back
soft voices, echoing around me
in the darkest lanes,
until I find myself
crumpled against the cobblestones
like a used cigarette,
my tip still a glowing ember
preparing to snuff itself out.

I remember the hurried footsteps,
gaze up at the sky as it calls my name—
the rain pushes against my lids,
forcing them to close.

Slowly I descend
out of all the repeated memories and haunted dreams;

out of all the burnt remains I once called by name;
out of everything I ever knew
but now alone demand.

I have made my cross of stone
so it would not wither
nor fade nor fall apart.
The surface is cold.
I stretch out my arms and wait.

The Night That Fell

With a harsh moon giving way to the sun
the sundogs glowed like prismed fires above.
The feral ones charged and moved silently into buildings
that swallowed the sun from the clouds and the clouds
from the rain—
to the gutter to the sewers to the oceans,
it all runs downhill to the end and the end
is near the start where we all were submerged.

Now it's all forgotten
with the rest of the centuries, asleep in the desert
where the flowers bloom as birds die,
watching the sound wither and fade.
Away in the distance I see a runner
sweating down mountains,
chasing boulders at its feet.

Is all the world laughing?
Or is it just the sky?

There ran rivers and sweet lilies and soft songs
that turned over the silence
like a warm blanket undoes the night.

The feral ones still charged,
clinging to their wallets as talismans
to ward off presumed evil
if evil cared about such things.

I watched a thick shadow pass
over the sundogs.
The feral ones assumed it was a cloud; a plane.

I look at water,
I see the dream of all that is liquid
in this dying world—
all that's chased to its sanctimonious closing
is pulling its way home
like the drawn tides.

All the rivers run here—
from this point time itself begins.
Here only clocks work and seconds
tick the days like soldiers on command.
The thin mist becomes rain
mingling with the ocean's waves—
said light which lights lights forever.

This land of visions and ghosts I find myself in—
I find the loss of words distracting.
But the flowers sing the song
whispered to them by the night that fell,
is falling
still.

Through Green Clouds

The clouds always seem so far away—
more distant, yet smaller, than fingertips—
somehow closer than trees.
Like clouds that puff up from riverbanks
where the highway cuts across,
oblivious in its concrete glory
to the chasms and light in the sky.

This netted life in its moment
seems relaxed among the green clouds—
the hillocks seem wistful in a way
that we are not.

Dreams come slowly—
sometimes it is not enough
to simply move on.

The Far Shore

At night sometimes the lake
sounds like it's right
outside my door,
breathing in the moonlight
like a soft cucumber condenses in the heat.

When those waves touch me
I lie back and hover in the night,
a starry darkened butterfly
caught on some current not seen.

Me here beneath the waves
holding my breath as I surface
to sparkles of sunlight on waves.

It's like my eyes opening for the first time
on a bright landscape of color and dreams—
to breathe fresh air for the first time.

All moments cease,
lead back to this pinpoint of time—
this single moment of certainty
that time will continue.

The music haunts me in its slow stillness—
sometimes I try to whisper back
but the waves enclose me
and my voice fades.

Songs & Ballads

Song of the Morning

Leaves like green sunflakes
waving to me from the canopy
where once they held mist
in veiny sharp fingers of bark and substance,
now capturing light like hope
between tendrils of spiderweb,
wings of morning flies, and dying mosquitoes.
All around, invisible birds sing—
they ride great boughs and small twigs
like tiny feathered surfers of the forest.

The dog, with tail down and nose straight—
sniffing the air, the grass, the leaves
for signs of life—
knows more of this than I.
She doesn't speak—
she looks, she listens,
she curls the air around her tail and waits,
pulling the leash like a hangman's noose,
wanting to move skyward into sun and mist.

We run down the road and try to jump,
but the roots pull us back
and we stay.

Song of the Fall

One of the thankless souls trudging
down long avenues of dead leaves
reflecting gold in sunlight that burns
through thick clouds like woodsmoke
hanging still in the air.

Along this corridor of thin light,
the streetlamps hung like pearls.
Above this highway airplanes hang in silence,
carrying some still further and faster.

There must be more to life than this strange play
of pens and paper and computer screens—
more than spinning tires.
Somehow the dead leaves know
as they strike sparks when falling
or cast back shadows to the moon.

I bide the time
until my return from the deep dark
sleep of clocking hours—
we fall to make the return
more sweet.

Ballad of Time

All these echoes repeat and dance—
a bowl of stars inverted over our heads.
The fish below dream of water, while we dream
of time and representations of time and events
to mark the passage of time. All this time time goes
nowhere.

This shadow's moment touches time like a beacon
burning brightly on the near shore of a far isle
where crystalline waves shatter
the stillness of the air—
the magpie's cries are all we have
to prove that shimmering glimpses exist.

This vacuum turns back hours from our nails.
The divine minutes drip
like scarlet silence holding its breath
against all the quiet memories batted away
like so much dew from leaves.

We drink that delicate redness;
fall into soft warm echoes of delight;
brandish ourselves in dark eyes wide open.

It all turns gray in the end, they say.
The slow, cold beckons of time wither,
the fading roses lose their color to silence in a starry sky—
all the ladders crumble,

all the climbers fall
beyond our out-stretched fingertips.

Song of the City

All these buildings, all this time
caught up in granite and steel
like wings caged before they can spread—
the quiet puff of daffodils unbloomed.
This future of wet streets and endless lights
bent backwards to touch each other where we hurt most.

When will the sadness end?
When will the cool dismay of desire
echo away in the past and leave us
to fend for ourselves?

After all the dreams have been built or trapped,
who will there be left to enjoy them?
What heartless wonder with no eyes will witness
the beauty of our time?

For the image of the world is this, my friend:
A great wheel turning endlessly
with no direction no center no form,
held tethered by the bodies of the faithful—
the empty words of leaders with fire in their eyes,
a dying ember of twice forgotten things
that know not how to pray or offer obedience.

This is the image of the world, old man.
I give it to you now for it is
all we have left to hold us together.

Song of the Stars

I am the sky that brings the water
and the fish that swim within.
I am the lamb that grew old and died
and the bull that ran with him.

I am two if I am one:
I am the crab in the harvest moon.
I am the lion dressed to kill
and the virgin he made swoon.

I am justice burning bright
and the snake lost in the night.
I am the wolf in the long black shell,
I am the hunter who kills so well.

Song of Today

This too shall pass, into dreams dispel—
the haze of a thousand days
lost in the night
to mongrel barks and hidden teeth
that flash in the moonlight and grow

With all placement of worldly worlds
in small hand baskets woven of tomorrow
and tomorrow—
the reflective surface of today
stretched tight across nightfall

Ballad of the City

The city seems quiet now
in all its hideous nature—
bright spear-headed phalluses
poke toward the clouds
like the rib cage of some mythic carcass.

Those homes nearest the remains
are dark and shuttered,
keeping the streets at bay—
a wall of sympathy
against which the festering disease of human nature
beats endlessly.

Those trapped inside,
I think of them—
of the sick waiting to die,
or of the healthy waiting to fall,
lit by the soft glows
of their televisions, watching
other worlds so they can ignore their own.

And I think,
it shouldn't be like this.

Song of Something

That she bends time to her will
is no disguise
for when she moves, time stops cold.

I have seen eyes as deep as hers
only in dreams where lavender tucks the corners
of a soft mattress back for movement.

She is the purity and beauty of a starry sky
blessed with a wisdom that reaches
further back than ever
mankind could hope to witness.

She came to me once,
drifting on a curtain of air—
to see her cheeks smile like that;
her smooth dark skin and many-colored raiment of white.

Something stirred in the air:
not her breath on my neck
nor her kisses on my cheek.

The delicate way her fingers held me—
her substance moved as her soul
burdened the weight of all
she cried for.

Something stirred—

some delicate substance burdened she
and she moved—
breathed her fire on my neck.

And I can't remember what it is.

Song of the Street

My man, my man,
we've been down this road before—
seen those stoplights swinging,
heard that creak of street signs in the wind.
We've seen all these ghosts
huddled at storefront windows
gazing at things they cannot afford.
We've watched the dead leaves
roll out of town, down by the river.

These tracks, they ain't nothing new—
we've seen them gleam in the sunlight,
laid pennies on that sheen and waited.
And how many times have we walked,
backs into the wind to keep the dust
from our eyes, planning some revenge
or simply talking, talking, but never
making a point?

We ain't old yet, but we've done all this before—
my footprint's still in that slab of sidewalk.
And how many people have said
they're gonna cross that river,
never to look back?

You and me, my man,
and we're still here.

Song of the Flag

The flag flutters,
sweeps stillness in the air.
I am reminded of something,
perhaps of her—
the way her hair flutters;
her legs sweep when she walks.

Dazed, I wonder up at the fabric
like a wounded head drooping again—
like pride rising up
only to hang limp.
Perhaps I am struck by a mood,
a calm wave in the haze—
the languid gait of early summer
when everyone has forgotten
how to open their windows,
let the breeze in,
sit in a chair like liquid
and just ooze through the day.

An out-of-season leaf dances
across the sidewalk before me—
I see it measure the distance,
hold my breath
as it moves across the street.

Perhaps I am thinking of movement;
of her walking home in the calm storm;

of us finally leaving—
our last goodbyes;
our lives.

People & Remembrances

Where the Waters Whisper

The silence of a home away from here:
the stillness of the summer hills as they turn back and shrug
snow from their trees.
The days tick past like hours,
watching the sun spin in its endless dance over oblivion;
the coolness of the drafts that appear near rattling windows.

Winter winds whip through springtime airs—
this promise comes undone,
leaves a growing season now cold
to pull pumpkins from vines and take me over there,
past the maple trees and snow-white hills, to you.

I think of us at home and wonder
why we remain so far from it all—
how we can shovel the crisp air,
full of fall leaves and drifting smoke,
under the promise of some distant future.

I see shadows where shapes ought to be.

Dead of Life

The chainsaw buzz of insects in
an early morning sun
as thunder laps above in
distant clouds that roll like butter.

I've seen all the moods of this season—
I know every wrinkle of summer's face—
but this, this is different,
an imbalance of the pure
light feather stroke of dawn
within.

There is nothing more wrong
than what we create.
Whispered voices may say otherwise,
but what do the dead know of life?
How quickly do they forget?

Drinking With Trees

When the clouds bend down to touch the treetops
people get scared
as if the intrusion from above was unwelcome—
as if the humidity and slow thunder were not harbingers
of the perfect light to come.

The people sit tight and panic, talking nervously,
trying to cover the sounds of birdsong which,
if they listened,
would tell them of the humid hum of early summer,
shaking off the shivers of winter
to make its presence known.

Somewhere out on a deep forest floor
the rains have already come.
The trees have said their thank-yous—
have shaken hands with the clouds
that soon enough will return
to the silence of their lofty mountains.

Eclipse

You have to let yourself go to it, find the weight and pull,
never mind the years and images,
just take the step and eclipse.

Let me walk now in time with time, for I am
here where I have never been before; we are
there where they will never see us again.

The hard pop of acorns on the roof
like the problems we imagine
being swayed, shaken free
from the things we have constructed.

Let me go over to it: the sweet solace and the lie.

Water

You are only ever wet now—
the way your eyes looked when you took in everything.
The way you roam and say you're sorry,
as if we've been here before,
as if this room is as familiar as your sentiment,
your truth, your escaping mouth and silent ohs.
As if the dismay could rain down swiftly and wash it all away.
As if you and I were wet like the delicate dew
you brushed away with your footprints in the grass—
a slow, long trail through greed and envy—
the kind you washed away like everything
is washed away in the end,
or so we think.

Lettering the Elements

There was a time somewhere
in the back of the long gone where
the people slipped by silently as if on wheels or ice,
passing by without looking,
hats pulled tight and collars high,
showing only a thin wedge of nose or a wayward wisp of hair.

Here once we played and I saw you move between the trees,
your pale face blossomed in the shadows then off,
away, further down—
the glittering sound of your laughter
like echoes of the rain at night.

It is a trapped sound that echoes
down chambers and along tunnels,
running ragged temptation in the night—
the flickers on the walls form shadows that don't exist.

I remember this: I was a witness to this glory,
the slow thaw and trickle of ice that became
a torrent, a creek, a river, a sea.
It all comes back to me now:
the slow, painful breaths; the missing time.

So then we walk, you and I and the trees
pass beside us and we move and the stars
wink and beckon until the cool air moves us
to leap.

Yet somewhere the melody lies and I stand
betrayed by the great escaping vision
of those things once yet to come
that never found their way.

All the Empty

This is where I ended.
All this for a smile.

The heart of the matter is the quickened fear,
the half-wide sway of forgotten lore,
the pieces kept furnished
of the banished road
of the painstaking ability
to always return home.

Walking down the street this midnight yesterday,
here is where we fold together—
moon cast your shadows,
moon cast away.

Tomorrow I will refabricate
my promises to you.
We will lie happily side by side,
each showing half our faces—
we've gone on too long
to finger the truth
any longer.

I'll come to you when everything is quiet.
I'll beg you again but you will come to me
in your own time.
I can't freeze all the days
or test time like a river—

Does it seem like reason to smile
at the sky folded open over me like a wet blanket,
with so many stars I cannot possibly
touch them all, but I may as well try?

This sour blemish turns me cold.
I know the only thing left
is dreaming here with me
not hanging from the backdrop of night
like the frigid blacktop of state route fifty west.

Not a lonely scrap of wisdom can prepare you for this,
nor all the rage of a thousand ages.
The way she looks at me—
sound-eyed and smiling—
can you look at me
without the fear you're hiding?
What will be left
this tomorrow yesterday?
Another empty bottle?
Another girl to betray?

In the Distance of the Stars

In a dry dawn
with the sun at my back,
thinking of you,
pleasing the pleasure
of a memory of you.
Am I not what I used to be?

All I can see between this thick rift
is the distance of the stars
between my home and yours.
This is not meant to be.
Sitting listening to the sirens drive by
to put out the fire
that will get me before too long.

First I must perform this play.
I have worked on the script too long
to perfect my lines
so it is untrue,
but that is me to you.

In the distance of the stars
I ask you to go
and you must refuse.

Rain Dance

"I think it's going to rain."
"Yes, that's what I thought you'd say."
Two old ladies and their sidewalk dog
passing evenly over the cracks.
One waves goodbye,
the other passes on without a look—
her white dog sniffs my leg.
They say the cool cock criminal
having eventually found a home
will stay.

The Hills

The hills were slippery
inebriated
I felt like I could jump
right into the sky—
watching the birds...

The pine trees in their silent majesty
the stars too perfect to be accidental
lances of light on the highway below—
the soft voice of cars driven in sadness

The fondness for the squeal of life
in the blackest silver-coated trees
black shadows lay like carpet
rolled out and out into mud puddles
into forever
for now

We darken and invite
these joys into our rooms

Slow Birth

Wind on the back of my neck
like a lover's breath
Dogs bark in the distance
awaiting the lightning beyond—
Tomorrow is wide
open for today

The scent of hyacinth
like its petals in the air—
All around the world is humming
but I
I sing here alone

Seeing an open grave—
I've tried and tried not to
pull myself in
This is death
death is here
I couldn't quite see
the worms inside the dirt

There is no end
no matter what they say
I could go on for days
feeling sorry for myself
hanging a foot over empty space
gazing down at not me
(I am sorry)

Death, death, death is
everywhere
I am
only here

The Great Heron Emerges from the Galactic Core

The skeletal claws of indifference
brandish a grim aspect:
there are never enough moments to feign surprise,
only horror.

When new ground is broken
the land is dark and the tigers all untied.
Life is built on recollection—
death comes short on the advent
of veiled insight.

There is no light in the darkness,
no turning back to retrace regretful steps.
Everything moves simply forward,
paved with the stones
of a thousand lonely aspects.

There is no memory to compare with this.

Becoming a Tree

Roots dug deep into firm ground,
looking for water—
leafless branches sway amid stars—
stony bark lifeless to the touch.

It begins with a splinter in your hand—
the dull aches of night throbbing
where once vigor kept muscles relaxed.
Arms out-stretched bend in the darkness and cold,
feet immovable by time,
like dew on grass that never fades away.

The slow fire finds fingers cracking,
bleeding sap and oozing regret
as rivers of streams propel the magic forward.
Somewhere the hawk finds purchase—
a shoulder, a foot buried in dirt, a backwards stare.

Things once of boredom now breed excitement—
the slow progress of life unfolds in an hour
when legs like stumps support a torso.
Eyes like knots survey the land,
see children and snowfall and sunrise.

The arms ache no longer.
Life solidifies as we turn now to autumn.

Over an Ageless Yesterday

And the moisture fades;
my brow softens as my shoes
turn for home.

I have forgotten the sound
of the delicate footsteps
that carried me here in the first place:
Through the saplings and the vines,
over rough bridges and trees,
through leaves silently rustling
in the shimmer of a moonless night.

I pull my hat down over my heart and wait,
watching for the sun to slowly rise and glimmer
beneath the tears on my face.

Widdershins

The house seems like winter:
The whitewash, the shutters,
the gray plate of sky behind.
Light crawls thinly from rooms
closed and curtained against the sky.
Cars shiver past on aching tires,
bit with fragile air.

The thinness extends, takes over
descriptions of everything,
turns the most stalwart of oaks
into shivering claws of bone
scratching the blank, sunless sky.

Somewhere they drift—
sun, moon, stars, you, and I—
apart from ice like concrete,
but clinging just as tight.

We freeze.
We shudder.
We call for home.

www.ingramcontent.com/pod-product-compliance
Lightning Source LLC
Chambersburg PA
CBHW020605030426
42337CB00013B/1218